NEW VANGUARD • 180

KAMIKAZE

Japanese Special Attack Weapons 1944–45

STEVEN J. ZALOGA   ILLUSTRATED BY IAN PALMER

First published in Great Britain in 2011 by Osprey Publishing,

Midland House, West Way, Botley, Oxford, OX2 0PH, UK

44–02 23rd St, Suite 219, Long Island City, NY 11101, USA

E-mail: info@ospreypublishing.com

A CIP catalog record for this book is available from the British Library

Print ISBN: 978 1 84908 353 9

PDF e-book ISBN: 978 1 84908 354 6

Page layout by Melissa Orrom Swan, Oxford
Index by Mike Parkin
Typeset in Sabon and Myriad Pro
Originated by United Graphic Pte
Printed in China through Worldprint Ltd

11 12 13 14 15   10 9 8 7 6 5 4 3 2 1

Osprey Publishing is supporting the Woodland Trust, the UK's leading woodland conservation charity by funding the dedication of trees.

www.ospreypublishing.com

AUTHOR'S NOTE

The author would especially like to thank Art Loder of IPMS-NENY and Brian Nicklas of the National Air & Space Museum library for their help with references for this book. Thanks also to Tom Laemlein for help with photos.

CONTENTS

KAMIKAZE
JAPANESE SPECIAL ATTACK WEAPONS 1944–45

INTRODUCTION

By the autumn of 1944, Japan was facing the defeat of its armed forces, and a likely American invasion of the Home Islands in 1945. In desperation, they turned to suicide weapons, the legendary *kamikaze*. Although kamikaze aircraft are the best known of these weapons, there was a variety of special attack naval options, including human torpedoes, crash boats, and frogmen. The army also had its own last-ditch weapons, such as antitank lunge mines.

A postwar American study of Japanese air power concluded that "the single most effective air weapon developed by the Japanese was the suicide plane." In contrast, the naval kamikaze weapons were more a dangerous nuisance than a serious threat to the US fleet. The special focus of this book is on the weapons designed in 1944–45 specifically for the special attack missions.

This dramatic image was taken seconds before this aircraft, probably a Yokosuka D4Y3 Suisei, narrowly missed the escort carrier USS *Sangamon* on May 4, 1945, off Kerama Retto, part of the 5th *Kikusui* wave. Moments later, the carrier was struck near the flight deck by another aircraft. (NARA)

ORIGINS OF THE KAMIKAZE – TOKKO

By the spring of 1944, the Imperial Japanese armed forces were on a precipitous slide to defeat. Any technological and tactical superiority enjoyed by the Imperial Japanese Navy (IJN) and Army (IJA) in 1941 had been eroded away by more than two years of war. This weakening was especially evident in the balance of air and naval power. In the hope of regaining a measure of tactical parity, a number of junior IJN and IJA officers in 1943 proposed a variety of suicide weapons, including crash boats, human torpedoes, and human-guided rocket bombs. There was widespread resistance to such extreme measures and concern that they would be unacceptable to the Emperor. Prior to the start of the official kamikaze campaign in the autumn of 1944, however, there had been occasional instances of Japanese aircraft crashing into US ships, dubbed *jibaku* attacks by Japanese pilots, but they were neither ordered nor organized by higher authorities.

The US amphibious landings in the Marianas, starting on June 15, 1944, penetrated Japan's inner defensive line and put US Army Air Force (USAAF) B-29 bombers within range of Japanese homeland. The IJN activated its *A-Go* plan, dispatching most of its surviving carrier force towards the Philippine Sea in hopes of a decisive naval battle that would reverse the course of the war in the Pacific. Instead, the IJN carrier aviation force was annihilated in the "Marianas Turkey Shoot" by the US Navy on June 19, 1944. The battle of the Philippine Sea clearly demonstrated that the IJN had lost the edge it previously had over US carrier aviation and the balance of air power had shifted irredeemably in favor of the Americans.

In mid 1944, secret discussions were held among senior Japanese commanders about using organized suicide attacks as a means to restore a Japanese advantage. Following the battle of the Philippine Sea, Rear Adm Obayashi, commander of the 3rd Carrier Division, volunteered to form suicide units. Due to the Emperor's ambivalent attitude towards this extreme tactic, the euphemism of "Tokko" (*Tokubetsu kogeki*: special attack) was used by the military for these tactics. In September 1944, the commanders of the IJA 4th Air Army and the IJN's 1st Air Fleet conducted a set of tests to examine bomber accuracy against ships in Manila harbor. The experiments concluded that only one in four well-trained crews would hit the target on

Japan's difficulties with advanced technologies accelerated the slide into desperate measures like the kamikaze. This is a Mitsubishi Ki-147 I-Go-1 Ko missile under a Mitsubishi Ki-67 Hiryu bomber, one of a number of failed attempts at developing guided anti-ship missiles. (NARA)

A Yokosuka D4Y3 Suisei bomber piloted by Lt Yoshinori Yamaguchi of the 701st Air Group moments before impacting on the deck of the carrier USS *Essex* on November 25, 1944, during the fighting in the Lingayen Gulf off the Philippines. The strike killed 15 and injured 44, but the carrier was back in action by mid December 1944. (NARA)

average, while the expectation was that even a modestly trained suicide pilot would hit his target every time. With the start of US amphibious landings on Leyte in October 1944, the focus of the new Tokko tactics centered on the Philippines.

The IJA began recruiting Tokko crews in July 1944 for two special units, which would be equipped with converted bombers armed with large warheads capable of sinking major warships. The Banda Squadron was formed around a dozen Ki-49-II Donryu (Storm Dragon, known by the Allied codename "Helen") bombers, and the Fugaku Squadron had the same number of Ki-67 Hiryu (Flying Dragon/"Peggy") bombers, both types fitted with special 1,760lb (800kg) warheads. These units did not arrive in the Philippines until October 24–25 owing to delays in converting the aircraft. As a stop-gap measure, the 4th Air Army in the Philippines organized improvised Tokko units by arming Ki-43 Hayabusa (Peregrine Falcon/"Oscar") fighters with bombs. Japanese Army accounts identify an attack on September 13, 1944, by two aircraft from the 31st Fighter Squadron from Los Negros and an attack by three fighters on September 21–22 as among the first authorized Tokko attacks. These claims remain controversial, however, and most accounts point to the navy missions a month later as the true start of the kamikaze missions.

On October 15, 1944, Rear Adm Masafumi Arima, commander of the 26th Air Flotilla in the Philippines, attempted to crash a Yokosuka D4Y Suisei (Comet/"Judy") bomber into a US carrier. A later Japanese account noted that "This act of self-sacrifice by a high flag officer spurred the flying units in forward combat areas and provided the spark that touched off the organized use of suicide attacks in the battle for Leyte." When Vice Adm Takijiro Onishi took over command of the IJN's 1st Air Fleet in the Philippines on October 17, 1944, he promptly began organizing the first IJN Tokko unit under his own initiative. Onishi, previously an opponent of Tokko tactics, argued that as long as the pilots were going to die in a combat operation, then their deaths should not be futile. Volunteers were sought from the ranks of the 201st Air Group in the Philippines to form the Shimpu Tokubetsu Kogekitai (Divine Wind Special Attack Unit), named after the typhoons that had wrecked the Mongol fleet during an attempted invasion of Japan in 1274. The "divine wind" ideogram can be pronounced either as "Shimpu" or "Kamikaze" while the former was used by Adm

A view of the USS *Essex* moments after the kamikaze impact on November 25, 1944, taken from the nearby USS *Langley*. (NARA)

Onishi, the later pronunciation was the more common form, and is the version used here.

The original IJN Tokko aircraft were ordinary Mitsubishi A6M5 Reisen ("Zero"/"Zeke") fighters stripped of armament, radios, and other unnecessary weight and armed with a 550lb (250kg) bomb. The only other change necessary was to fit wiring that permitted the pilot to activate the bomb's arming system for detonation on impact. (Tactics soon changed to encourage the pilot to release the bomb prior to impact with the hope of damaging the warship at two points.)

A single IJN suicide mission was launched on October 21, 1944, and the cruiser HMAS *Australia* was hit and damaged, though possibly by one of several scattered IJA Tokko attacks. The first large IJN Tokko mission, however, took place on October 25, 1944, sinking the US escort carrier *St. Lo* and damaging the carrier USS *Santee* off the Philippines. The success of this small group of aircraft validated the Tokko concept in the eyes of many commanders. On October 30, therefore, the Emperor received the navy minister, Adm Mitsumasa Yonai, and remarked: "It is truly regrettable that it should be necessary to go to this extreme, but they have done well." These remarks were taken by the IJN as the Emperor's tacit approval for the Tokko missions. Onishi was instructed to form the Dai-Ichi Rengo Kichi Kokubutai (First Combined Basic Attack Group) in the Philippines to conduct further Tokko operations. Since the Japanese air forces in the Philippines had been decimated in previous air actions, numerous reinforcements were dispatched, primarily from IJN units on Taiwan.

Although the initial IJN Tokko attacks were conducted using fighters, the tactics were soon extended to most other types of aircraft, including navy dive-bombers such as the D4Y3 Suisei and medium bombers such as the P1Y1 Ginga (Milky Way/"Frances"). The army focused on conventional air attacks through October, but by the end of November it was clear that the navy Tokko tactics were far more successful, and they encouraged the army to switch to suicide attacks as well. The Banda Squadron lost all but four of its converted Ki-49-II Kai aircraft on the ground to American air attacks, but launched its first attack on November 12 against ships in Leyte Gulf. This mission was a failure, despite claims that a battleship and transport had been sunk. The Fugaku Squadron conducted its first mission with five converted Ki-67-I Kai To-Go on November 13, 1944, again without success. Its two

The Ki-67-I Kai To-Go was a Tokko version of the Hiryu bomber fitted with a pair of 1,760lb (800kg) warheads. The nose-mounted probe contained a fuze to ensure the detonation of the warhead. The aircraft was first used in combat by the Fugaku Squadron during the Philippines campaign, but this example was found at Clark Field on Luzon after the fighting. (NARA)

final missions were on January 10 and 12, 1945, and they may have been responsible for damaging the destroyer USS *Le Ray Wilson* on January 10.

Five more Ki-67-I *Kai To-Go* conversions were completed in Japan in December 1944 and sent to the Philippines for the depleted Banda Squadron. Other specially organized army Tokko units soon joined the attacks, starting with the Yasukuni and Hakko Squadrons in late November 1944, using ordinary fighters and attack aircraft like their navy counterparts. Tokko attacks began to peter out at the end of 1944, after the Japanese had exhausted their air fleets in the Philippines.

During the course of the Philippines fighting from October 1944 to January 1945, a total of 421 IJN Tokko aircraft sortied, of which 378 were expended; they were supported by 239 escort fighters, of which 102 were shot down, crashed, or were otherwise lost. The army sent out 400 aircraft on 61 Tokko missions. The IJN claimed to have struck 105 ships, while the IJA posted results of 154 hits, the combined figure being more than double the actual results. Japanese pilots claimed to have sunk 37 warships including five carriers and seven battleships or cruisers. Actual losses were 16 ships and boats of all types sunk, including two escort carriers and three destroyers. About 45 percent of the sorties were downed by US Navy Combat Air Patrols (CAPs); of those aircraft that made it past the fighters, about 46 percent were shot down by naval antiaircraft fire. Tokko aircraft scored 121 hits and 53 damaging near-misses, delivered by 22 percent of the Tokko aircraft taking part. Regardless of the precise figures, the kamikazes proved to be the most destructive and effective element of Japanese air power during the Philippines campaign.

In the wake of the Philippines campaign, IJA and IJN commanders held a number of conferences, which concluded that the Tokko attacks were the

A **SPECIAL ATTACK BOMBERS**
1: KI-49-II KAI DONRYU, BANDA SQUADRON, PHILIPPINES, DECEMBER 1944
2: KI-167 SAKURA-DAN, FUGAKU SQUADRON, OKINAWA, MAY 1945
The converted Ki-49-II Donryu were assigned to the special attack Banda Squadron, formed from the 74th and 95th Squadrons of the IJA's 4th Air Army. The aircraft shown here is in the markings of the 74th Sentai. The Ki-167 Sakura-dan of the 62nd Squadron attached to the Fugaku Squadron was marked with the *Hoo* emblem on the tail, a stylized representation of a mythical peacock-like bird that materializes when peace and holiness prevail. This particular example was flown by 2nd Lt Yukata Fukushima on the May 25, 1945, mission near Okinawa. The aircraft were finished in a non-standard dark blue-gray.

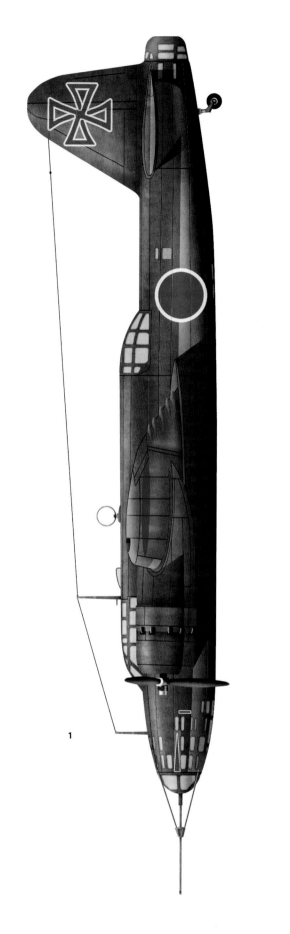

1

2

A remarkable view of the approach of an A6M5 Zero fighter towards the battleship USS *New Mexico* on January 6, 1945, off San Fernando in the Lingayen Gulf. The aircraft struck the port side of the bridge moments later. The strike killed the ship's captain Robert Fleming and Winston Churchill's representative with Gen. MacArthur's HQ, LtGen Herbert Lumsden, along with 29 others, as well as injuring 87 crewmen. (NARA)

best aerial tactic yet attempted by either arm, and that the only way to stop the next US amphibious operation was by a concentrated and combined Tokko campaign. The conferences also decided that a certain number of fighters had to be withheld from suicide missions to provide escort cover to defend against US Navy combat air patrols, and that the most effective tactic was to concentrate the Tokko aircraft in a single wave to saturate and overwhelm the US Navy defenses. The policy of depending on volunteer pilots was quietly dropped and a few units relied on compulsory recruitment.

Due to the heavy losses of Japanese aircraft in the Philippines, neither the IJA nor IJN were ready for a Tokko campaign at the time of the US landings on Iwo Jima on February 19, 1945. Only a single combined mission involving 25 Tokko aircraft (21 IJN and 4 IJA) was launched on February 21, sinking the escort carrier USS *Bismarck Sea* and damaging the carriers *Saratoga* and *Lunga Point*, as well as three other ships. From February 14 to the start of the Okinawa campaign on March 5, there were 259 Tokko sorties, of which

The cruiser USS *Colombia* under attack around 1724hrs on January 6, 1945, in the Lingayen Gulf by a Mitsubishi Ki-51 attack aircraft of the 6th Hakko/Sekicho Squadron, 4th Air Army. The aircraft's bomb penetrated two decks before exploding, killing 13 people and wounding 44. The cruiser remained in action and was hit again on January 9. (NARA)

10

131 aircraft were expended. Most of these missions were flown against US fleet operations in the waters off southern Japan, but no ships were sunk. The most ambitious Tokko attack during this period was Operation *Tan No. 2*, an attempt to strike the US fleet anchorage at the Ulithi Atoll. The Azusa Tokkotai of the 762nd Naval Air Group consisting of 24 P1Y1 Ginga bombers left Kanoya on the morning of March 11. During their dusk attack, a Ginga damaged the carrier USS *Randolph*.

TOKKO DURING THE OKINAWA CAMPAIGN

The IJN focused its next major kamikaze effort on Operation *Ten-Go*, the defense of Okinawa. During this campaign, both the IJN's 5th Air Fleet and the IJA's 6th Air Army were under navy control, as an attempt at a more unified tactical approach, with Vice Adm Matome Ugaki in command of the First Mobile Base Air Force. These units were based mainly on Kyushu in southern Japan. The massed Tokko attacks were codenamed as *Kikusui* (Floating Chrysanthemum) and numbered sequentially. *Kikusui* became the iconic emblem of the Tokko campaign due to its association with the legendary warrior Kusunoki Masashige. After a heroic but futile defense during the battle of Minatogawa in 1336, Kusunoki committed ritual suicide rather than surrender, uttering the famous slogan: "I wish only that I could be reborn seven times to fight my Emperor's enemies." "Seven lives for the Emperor" became the battle-cry of the Tokko force; Kusunoki's emblem, the *Kikusui*, became its symbol.

Okinawa was by far the largest and most successful Tokko campaign of the war. It started on March 26, 1945, on a small scale, and followed on April 6 and 7 with the first major wave attack, involving almost 729 Tokko aircraft and escort fighters. This mission was one of the largest Japanese air operations of the entire war. During the Okinawa campaign, the army missions were flown mainly by single-engine fighter and attack aircraft, with the Ki-27 "Nate" (150), Ki-43 "Oscar" (120), Ki-51 "Sonia" (11), Ki-61 "Tony" (60), and Ki-84 "Frank" (60) being the predominant types.

The battleship USS *Tennessee* moments after being struck by an IJN Aichi D3A Kanbaku ("Val") dive-bomber of the 2nd *Kikusui* wave off Okinawa on April 12, 1945 with its bomb penetrating below deck into the warrant officers' quarters amidships on the starboard side with 22 killed and 107 wounded. (NARA)

The table below summarizes the attacks. Besides the main *Kikusui* waves, some small-scale raids were also conducted, and there was a separate and distinct set of attacks staged from Taiwan via the island bases of Sakishima Gunto. The IJN exaggerated its victories during the Okinawa offensive, claiming to have sunk 44 ships, including two carriers and eight battleships, while in fact sinking 17 ships including one escort carrier and 11 destroyers, and damaging 279 other vessels. During the Okinawa fighting, nearly a quarter of US warships were hit by a kamikaze.

Okinawa Campaign Tokko Attacks				
Mission	**Date (1945)**	**IJN**	**IJA**	**Total**
Kikusui 1	April 6/7	230	125	355
Kikusui 2	April 12/13	125	60	185
Kikusui 3	April 15/16	120	45	165
Kikusui 4	April 27/28	65	50	115
Kikusui 5	May 3/4	75	50	125
Kikusui 6	May 10/11	70	80	150
Kikusui 7	May 24/25	65	100	165
Kikusui 8	May 27/28	60	50	110
Kikusui 9	June 3/7	20	30	50
Kikusui 10	June 21/22	30	15	45
Additional sorties	April–June	140	45	185
Taiwan sorties	April–June	50	200	250
Totals		1,050	850	1,900

Tokko effectiveness

In total, the IJN conducted about 64 percent of all Tokko attacks, and the IJA the remaining 36 percent. During the ten months of the kamikaze attacks, the Tokko missions accounted for 48.1 percent of all damaged US warships, and 21.3 percent of those sunk. These missions expended about 2,500 aircraft and 3,860 aircrew, and scored 474 hits on Allied warships, for an effectiveness rate per sortie of 18.6 percent. US, Australian, and British naval casualties during the kamikaze attacks included more than 7,000 killed.

A US Navy study of the Okinawa campaign concluded that about 10 percent of Tokko aircraft that set off on a sortie had to return to base due to mechanical problems, weather, or failure to locate a target. About half of those reaching the combat area were shot down by CAPs. Only about a third of those that escaped CAPs survived the naval antiaircraft fire and actually hit a ship. Overall, kamikaze aircraft were judged to be seven to ten times more effective per sortie than conventional aircraft attacks. A postwar US Navy assessment concluded that Tokko strikes were more effective than ordinary bomb hits, but substantially

A group of Tokko pilots hold a brief ceremony before their mission. This event was re-enacted at Chofu airbase in Japan in November 1945 for a film about the kamikaze movement. (NARA)

less effective than torpedo hits. Further naval studies indicated that the bombs on board the kamikaze were not the main cause of damage, but more often the resulting fires caused in large measure by exploding aircraft fuel.

Kamikaze Effectiveness vs. Aircraft Carriers

Weapon	Carriers requiring repairs (%)	Weeks in yard	Weeks out of operation
Bomb	40	0.3	0.7
Kamikaze	70	1.8	4.3
Submarine torpedo	100	10	12.4
Aerial torpedo	100	10	17.5

The US Navy reacted to the kamikaze with new tactics and new technologies that dampened the effectiveness of the Tokko. Destroyers and destroyer escorts were used to establish picket lines around carrier task forces, serving both to extend the radar early-warning network and create a first line of defense against the kamikazes. These picket ships bore the brunt of the kamikaze casualties, because inexperienced Japanese pilots tended to attack the first warship they encountered. During the Okinawa campaign, therefore, destroyers constituted 11 of the 17 lost ships and 109 of the 198 ships and craft that were damaged. The picket ships provided additional time for Navy CAPs to intercept incoming kamikaze flights, and the fighters remained the most lethal antidote to Tokko attacks. The Philippines campaign had also led to a Navy program to increase the number of antiaircraft weapons on ships, and also hastened the deployment of proximity fuzes in antiaircraft shells, which significantly enhanced large-caliber air defense gunfire. The effectiveness of kamikaze attacks therefore decreased between the Philippines campaign and the battle off Okinawa due to both US Navy improvements in gunnery and the declining quality of Japanese aircrews. In the Philippines, about 54 percent of the kamikaze who made it through the CAPs scored a hit or near miss on a ship, but only 32 percent at Okinawa.

One of the final Tokko missions of the war was Operation *Arashi* (Storm), an attempt in August 1945 to launch Aichi M6A Seiran (Mountain Haze) of the Shinryu Tokubetsu Kogekitai (Divine Dragon Special Attack Unit) from the aircraft-carrying submarine I-400 and I-401 against the US fleet anchorage at Ulithi. The submarines were underway as the war ended, and this Seiran is now on display at the Udvar-Hazy Center of the Smithsonian National Air and Space Museum outside Washington DC. (Author)

Kamikaze Damage by Type of Ship					
	Attacking aircraft	Hits	Hits per attack (%)	Ships sunk	Sinking per hit (%)
Battleships	37	12	32	0	0
Cruisers	42	15	35	0	0
Fleet carriers	30	10	33	0	0
Light carriers	10	2	20	0	0
Escort carriers	39	15	33	2	13
Destroyers	303	92	30	12	13
Auxiliary/landing ships	428	121	28	25	20
Merchant ships	55	29	52	6	20
Totals	944	296	31% average	45	15% average

TOKKO IN THE FINAL DEFENSE OF JAPAN

The declining performance of the IJN and IJA air arms in the final year of the war convinced senior Japanese commanders that Tokko tactics were their last hope in the final defense of Japan. Consequently, kamikazes figured prominently in the plan for the final battle, Operation *Ketsu-Go*.

By the summer of 1945, there were few illusions about the ability of the IJA and IJN to prevent US amphibious landings on the Japanese coast. The strategic objective, therefore, was to inflict such severe losses on the American invaders that the United States would be willing to conduct political negotiations to bring about an end of the war, short of unconditional surrender. A conference at 6th Air Army headquarters in July 1945 concluded that Tokko missions could make a decisive contribution to repulsing the American naval landings, and would sink a third to a half of the invasion force. These estimations were in part based on grossly exaggerated assessments of the casualties already caused by the Tokko attacks. Japanese assessments were a mixture of poor information compounded by wishful thinking and propaganda efforts to justify the sacrifice of so many pilots. The erroneous predictions also diverted Japanese attention away from the technical lessons of the Okinawa campaign, in which most Tokko aircraft had a very low probability of sinking a warship even if they hit it. The ordnance carried on the aircraft, typically 550lb (250kg) bombs, were too small to guarantee the sinking even of small warships like destroyers, and were less effective against larger warships such as cruisers or battleships. The army suspected this to be the case, which was its reason for trying to convert bombers into Tokko aircraft with large warheads. Shortcomings in Tokko aircraft would only be exacerbated by the growing reliance on smaller planes for Tokko missions, such as trainers, that could not carry a powerful payload.

A common scene at many Japanese airbases in the weeks after the war was the removal of propellers from any aircraft that might be used for unauthorized kamikaze missions after the ceasefire. This is Atsugi airbase outside Tokyo, displaying a variety of IJN aircraft including Ginga and Suisei bombers. A final Tokko mission of the war was flown by Adm Matome Ugaki in a D4Y4 of the 701st Air Group from Oita airbase on August 15 after the Emperor's surrender announcement. (NARA)

IJN commanders hoped to stop the US invasion fleet by the sheer volume of Tokko attacks. By the summer of 1944, the IJN had about 4,300 trainer aircraft in Japan that would be converted to the Tokko role. This figure included not only dedicated primary trainers and advanced trainers, but also obsolete fighters such as the Zero, which were now being used in the trainer role. In addition, 700 dive-bombers, torpedo-bombers, medium bombers, and other attack aircraft would be allotted to the Tokko force. The most modern fighters such as the Raiden ("Jack") and Shiden ("George") were initially withheld from the Tokko force on the presumption that escorts would be needed; likewise reconnaissance aircraft were also exempted. Eventually, however, all aircraft would be expended in Tokko attacks.

The army air brigades had a smaller force in Japan for the *Ketsu-Go* plan than the navy. Conversion of obsolete aircraft types, especially the Ki-43 Type 1 fighters, began in late 1944 and about 800 were ready by April 1945. By the end of the war, the army had only about 800 operational fighters and bombers and about 2,100 dedicated kamikaze aircraft in Japan and the neighboring air sectors. These were split between the 1st Air Army in the Tokyo area (600 kamikaze aircraft), 6th Air Army headquartered at Fukuoka (1,000), and the 5th Air Army headquartered at Seoul in Korea (500). Since the objective was to sink 500 American transport ships, plans were made to increase the inventory of Tokko aircraft by producing at least 2,000 new dedicated Tokko models such as the navy's rocket-powered Ohka flying bomb (see below), and the army's more conventional Tsuragi.

A July 1945 conference estimated that about 60 percent of the available navy force would actually be operational at the time of the American landings and that of the 2,400 taking part about one in six, or 400 aircraft, would score hits. The army argued more optimistically that one in three of its aircraft would score hits, since the targets would be in the crowded transport areas, not against a dispersed fleet with heavy antiaircraft protection as had been the case in the Philippines and Okinawa battles.

Although Tokko aircraft were the primary form of kamikaze weapon for *Ketsu-Go*, the navy also had a broad array of Tokko naval craft and submarines that will be detailed later in this book.

SPECIALIST TOKKO AIRCRAFT

Aside from expedient aircraft conversions, there were a number of more elaborate conversion attempts to improve the performance of the Tokko attacks. As mentioned earlier, the army pioneered these efforts with the bomber conversions for the Banda and Fugaku Squadrons. The next Ki-67 Hiryu

A Nakajima Ki-9 Akatombo (Red Dragonfly/"Spruce") trainer at Kikuchi airbase outside Nagasaki in Japan in 1945, crudely prepared for a Tokko mission with a drum of gasoline in the rear cockpit. It has been painted with a typical emblem of the Tokko force, the cherry blossom, and the inscription on the tale includes the Kana symbol "To" from Tokko, and the Kazekaoru inscription "Rise on a perfumed breeze, fall in a rain of cherry blossoms." (NARA)

One of the lesser-known Tokko modification efforts was the development of this ventral fairing for modifying light bombers for kamikaze missions. It was designed to carry a 1,760lb (800kg) warhead, and had special fittings for four booster rockets to accelerate the aircraft during the terminal dive. (NARA)

conversion was more elaborate, incorporating the secret *Sakura-dan* (Cherry Blossom) shaped-charge warhead. This warhead was another case of German technical influence, as it was related to the SHL-3500 Beethoven warhead used on the Mistel guided bomb. A hollow-charge warhead was far more effective against armored ships than conventional blast warheads. However, its 5ft 3in diameter required a more substantial modification, with a plywood dorsal bulge added to the aircraft.

The conversion effort began in December 1944, but was continually delayed – the first five were completed by February 1945. Nicknamed "hunchbacked wizard grannies" by the crews, these Ki-167 Sakura-dan aircraft were deployed with the 62nd Squadron at Kanoya airbase in Kagoshima prefecture along with a small number of the Ki-67-I Kai To-Go conversions. One aircraft took part in an attempted attack on the US fleet around Okinawa on April 17, 1945, in the company of two Kai To-Go, but suffered a premature mid-air detonation of its warhead near Kikaijima, forcing a delay while the cause was investigated. Two other Sakura-dan were expended on a raid near Naha, Okinawa, on May 25 with unknown results, and there were unfulfilled plans to use additional aircraft of this type against Saipan in August 1945.

The IJN placed more of its hopes in new-build Tokko aircraft such as the Ohka, and some Zero fighters were also manufactured specifically as Tokko aircraft under the codename *Kembu*, these being able to carry a 1,100lb (500kg) bomb instead of the usual 550lb (250kg) bomb. These were issued mainly to elite Tokko units such as the *Jinrai* squadrons. Some late production Yokosuka D4Y4 Suisei bombers were modified to carry three solid rocket boosters under the rear fuselage to increase the speed of the aircraft during the terminal kamikaze dive.

B **OHKA LAUNCH FROM MITSUBISHI G4M2E TYPE 1 ISSHIKI ATTACK BOMBER MODEL 24 TEI**

The Ohka Type 11 was launched from a slightly modified version of the widely used Mitsubishi G4M2e Type 1 Isshiki Attack Bomber, better known to the Allies by its codename "Betty." The bomb-bay doors were removed, and a simple launch frame was fitted inside. In addition, the bomb-bay floor was modified to accommodate the cockpit canopy of the Ohka and to permit the Ohka pilot to enter and exit the aircraft in flight. This particular aircraft was originally a standard Model 24 Hei variant, converted to Model 24 Tei standards with the addition of a surface-search radar, evident from the antenna on the nose. This illustration shows the G4M2e in the markings of the 3rd Section, 711th Attack Squadron, 721st Navy Aviation Group, which was operating from Konoike airbase in March 1945. It was the 1st and 2nd Squadrons of this unit that conducted the ill-fated attack of March 21, 1944, when all of the bombers were shot down. The three squadrons in this unit can be identified by the tail flash, with the 1st having one flash, the 2nd two flashes, and the 3rd three flashes.

The MXY7 Ohka was a simple, rocket-powered glide bomb developed at the navy's Kugisho facility in Yokosuka. (NARA)

The Ohka

The most important of the custom-designed Tokko aircraft was the Ohka (Cherry Blossom) rocket-assisted glide bomb. This project had been proposed in 1943 by a transport pilot, Ensign Mitsuo Ohta. His ideas were ignored until the spring of 1944, when he was sent back to Japan to brief navy officials. His design was refined by Prof Taichiro Ogawa of the University of Tokyo, who drew up preliminary plans. His effort did not attract formal navy support until after the Marianas defeat in June 1944.

The project was transferred to the Kugisho (Kaigun-Koku-Gijutsu-Sho: Naval Air Technical Arsenal) at Yokosuka, and it formally began on August 16, 1944, codenamed Project *Marudai* under Cmdr Masao Yamana. The original scheme was to power the glider using a KR-10 liquid-fuel rocket engine being developed at Mitsubishi's Nagasaki plant on the basis of the German Walther rocket engine used in the Me-163 rocket fighter. This idea was quickly rejected due to the immaturity of the rocket engine, as well as its cost and complexity. Instead, the design switched to the use of available solid rocket boosters. The propulsion system was intended to be only enough to accelerate the aircraft during its final dive, since it would carried into the combat area by a larger bomber. The requirements focused on a simple aircraft made of wood and non-strategic materials and one that was easy to assemble and a tenth the cost of a conventional fighter. The Mitsubishi G4M2e Isshiki ("Betty") bomber was adapted for the deployment mission due to its widespread availability and adequate size.

The Ohka Model 11 was based around a massive 2,645lb (1,200kg) Tekkou armor-piercing warhead in the nose of the aircraft, as seen here on Okinawa with the nose fairing removed. (NARA)

The final production batches of Ohka aircraft had a metal fairing at the rear of the cockpit canopy, instead of the clear section on the earlier production run. This particular example was part of an Ohka unit being stored at Kawaya near Nagasaki at the end of the war. (NARA)

The first unpowered prototypes of the Ohka were completed in early September 1944, and in parallel the Ohka K-1 training version was also developed without rockets but with a skid landing gear. Static firing tests of the rocket motor began later in September. An unmanned Ohka was dropped over Sagami Bay on October 23, 1944, and the first manned test flight of an Ohka K-1 was conducted on October 31, 1944, using two wing-mounted rockets for propulsion. This flight was successful enough that series production of 45 Ohka K-1 trainers began immediately. The first successful test of a rocket-powered Ohka Type 11 took place on November 19, 1944. As a result, production of the type was authorized to begin under the designation MXY7, with 155 assembled at the Kugisho and 600 more at the Naval Air Arsenal at Kasumigaura although most of the main assemblies came from the Fuji Aircraft Co. near Hiratsuka and Nippon Hikkoki at Tomioka.

The original propulsion configuration for the Ohka was five solid rocket boosters, three in the rear fuselage and one under each wing. The wing-mounts were abandoned after the October 31 test flight and a second static ground test on November 19 when it was realized that they caused steering problems due to uneven burn rates and the resulting asymmetric thrust. This was not a problem on the fuselage rockets, since they were so near the centerline. The first Ohka, such as those deployed to Okinawa, were issued with all five rockets.

An elite Ohka unit, the Jinrai Butai (Divine Thunder Corps), was formed in September 1944 under Capt Motoharu Okamura, more formally designated as the 721st Naval Squadron. The unit was based at Konoike airbase in Ibaraki Prefecture and began training with the arrival of Ohka K-1 trainers. Only experienced pilots were accepted for the unit, and they were given an initial test flight from an altitude of 9,000ft (2,743m) and two more from 16,000ft (4,877m), at which point they were considered combat qualified.

The first 50 Ohka Type 11 aircraft were delivered to the aircraft carrier *Shinano* in Yokosuka in November 1944 for deployment to the Philippines, but the carrier was

The Ohka K1 was the basic training version of the Ohka and was fitted with a skid under the nose for the return landing. This hanger at Yokosuka is filled with the trainers. (NARA)

Specifications

Crew	1 pilot
Allied codename	Viper; Baka (popular nickname)
Length	20ft (6.09m)
Wingspan	16ft 5in (5m)
Weight	4,416lb (2,005kg)
Propulsion	Glider with three electrically ignited Type 4 Mark 1 Mod 20 rockets
Fuel	500 Special FDT-6 monoperforated, double-base solid propellant
Rocket thrust	1,500lb (680kg) average, 4,500 lb (2,040kg), maximum, 9.7-second duration
Warhead	Tekkou armor-piercing steel case warhead
Warhead fuzes	A-3 nose fuze, Model 1 base impact fuze, and Model 2 all-way action fuze
Warhead weight	2,645lb (1,200kg) with 1,135lb (515kg) of Type 91 trinitroanisol explosive
Range	max. 55 miles (88km) when released from 27,000 ft (8,230m); average ranges in combat were 4–6 miles (6–11km)
Speed	540–600mph (870–965km/h) in terminal

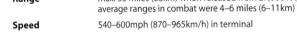

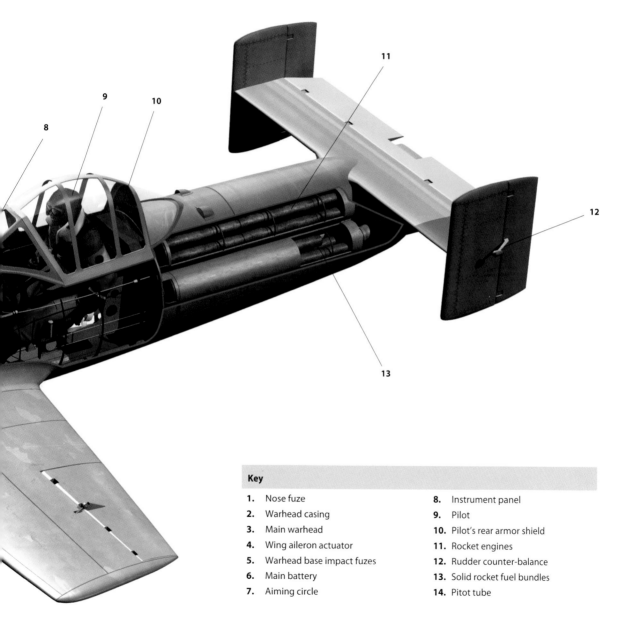

Key

1. Nose fuze
2. Warhead casing
3. Main warhead
4. Wing aileron actuator
5. Warhead base impact fuzes
6. Main battery
7. Aiming circle
8. Instrument panel
9. Pilot
10. Pilot's rear armor shield
11. Rocket engines
12. Rudder counter-balance
13. Solid rocket fuel bundles
14. Pitot tube

The Ohka K2 trainer was the only version of the Model 43 to enter production and can be distinguished both by its twin canopy configuration but also by the extended wings. This particular example was found at the Kugisho facility in Yokosuka at the end of the war. (NARA)

sunk on November 28 by the submarine USS *Archerfish*. Plans to deploy the Jinrai Butai to the Philippines in December were frustrated when the carrier *Unryu* that was supposed to deliver them was sunk by the submarine USS *Redfish* on December 19. A second Ohka unit, the 722nd Tatsumaki (Tornado Corps) Naval Squadron, was raised for new versions of the Ohka, but ended up reinforcing the existing Jinrai Butai when the new Ohka types failed to reach production. Plans to use the Ohka in the Iwo Jima campaign in February 1945 were frustrated when a pre-emptive US air attack against the Konoike base destroyed all 24 modified Betty bombers. The Ohka were first identified at Konioke by US intelligence on March 8, 1945, and given the codename "Viper."

The first combat sortie by the 721st Naval Squadron took place on March 21 from Kanoya airbase on Kyushu, carried by 16 G4M2 bombers of the 711th Attack Squadron and under the command of LtCdr Goro Nonaka. The Ohka force included two more bombers with conventional bombloads, and it was escorted by about 30 A6M5 fighters. Their target was US Task Force 58 operating off Kyushu, but when they were about 60 miles from their targets, they were intercepted by 24 US Navy fighters – F4U Corsairs of VF-17 and F6F Hellcat fighters of VBF-17 from USS *Hornet*. In just a few minutes every single bomber was shot down, along with most of the escort force.

The vulnerability of the Ohka/Isshiki combination to enemy fighters was well appreciated before the ill-fated March 21 mission, and the Kugisho had warned navy commanders that Ohka was only viable in the absence of enemy fighters or with heavy escort. Two steps were taken to address this problem. To begin with, tactics were changed so that Ohka/Isshiki combinations were dispatched singly or in very small groups to avoid detection and intercept by US Navy air patrols. In addition, work was already underway on other versions of the Ohka, the Model 21 and Model 22.

The Ohka Model 22 did not enter service due to problems with its engine. This example was restored at the Udvar-Hazy Center at the US National Air & Space Museum. (Author)

The Model 21 was a smaller version of the basic Model 11, with the warhead reduced to 1,320lb (600kg) and the wingspan shortened so that it could be carried by the faster P1Y1 Ginga bomber. This type was never produced. Instead, design shifted to the jet-powered Ohka Model 22, which was fitted with a Hitachi Tsu-11 jet engine, based on the Campini powerplant that first flew in Italy in 1941. The novel engine would allow the Ohka to be released from the Ginga bomber at a greater distance from the target, as much as 80 miles (130 km), increasing the survivability of both the Ohka and parent aircraft. Development of the Model 22 began on February 15, 1945, but was delayed due to the immaturity of the Tsu-11. In spite

The Ohka Model 22 was fitted with a Hitachi Tsu-11, a primitive type of jet engine that used a conventional Hatsukaze 150hp (112kW) gasoline-powered engine, as seen here, to drive a single-stage axial compressor behind it, which is missing in this view. (NARA)

of its unproven performance, limited production of 50 aircraft began at Yokosuka in the summer of 1945, even before a successful test flight. About 20 Tsu-11 engines were produced before the war ended, so few aircraft were completed. The first drop test was conducted on June 26, 1945, but ended in tragedy when the wing-mounted rocket boosters accidentally ignited on launch, precipitating a collision with the Ginga and a subsequent crash. The wing rockets were deleted, but another flight test on August 12 was abruptly terminated when the jet engine prematurely ignited before separation.

In the meantime, other propulsion options were studied. Besides the Tsu-11, the more advanced Ne-20 axial-flow turbojet was being developed for the Kikka jet fighter and was a smaller version of the BMW-003 used by the German Me-262 fighter. The Ohka Model 33 with this engine was planned for launch from the G8N1 Renzan ("Rita") heavy bombers and the Ohka Model 33 Ko version from submarine catapults. Design of this variant, however, was never completed as it was decided to proceed instead to a more radical solution, the Model 43.

Although powered by the Ne-20 like the Model 33, the Model 43 had extended wings to avoid the need for a parent bomber altogether. The Model 43A was intended for launch from a submarine or aircraft carrier, while the Model 43B was designed for launch from land-based coastal launchers. In

The Ohka Model 43 was delayed because of shortages of its NE-20 turbojet engine which was also used by the Kikka jet fighter. This wooden mock-up was found after the war in the Yokosuka workshops with an engine-compartment mock-up on the ground. (NARA)

The Ohka Model 43B was intended to be launched from special coastal bases. The Ohka was stored in a protective cave, and then rolled out to the launch rail on its special launch cart. The cart was propelled along the launch-rail by two rocket boosters. (Author)

parallel with the Model 43, the Ohka K-2 trainer was designed and ten were built in Yokosuka in May–June 1945 for preliminary training.

Design of the Ohka Model 43 was completed on April 26, 1945, and a wooden mock-up finished in May 1945; production tooling work started at Yokosuka and at Aichi Aircraft, but was disrupted by B-29 bomber attacks. Construction of the first Ohka Type 43 launch base began in July 1945 on the Miura peninsula, and there were plans to construct 41 launchers and 245 underground shelters at seven sites by mid October 1945. A catapult launch site was in operation at Takeyama near Yokosuka for training Ohka 43 pilots using the Ohka K-2 glider and the first test of a catapult using a K-2 trainer took place on June 27. A wooden mock-up of the Model 43B was tested on a catapult at the Mt Hiei site in August 1944. Yet the war ended before Ohka Model 43 production began. Another derivative of the Model 43 was also planned, the Model 53, which was intended to be towed into the air like a sailplane by another aircraft before igniting the engine and proceeding to the target. This variant never proceeded beyond the preliminary design stage.

Since none of the advanced Ohka types reached production, missions continued with the Ohka/Isshiki combination on March 21, 1945, during the campaign around Okinawa. A sortie by three bombers on April 1 was ineffective, and the same day, US Marines first discovered the secret Ohka from a cache of 15 near Kadena airbase on the island. It was dubbed the "Baka" (Fool) after its discovery on April Fool's Day.

On April 12, the Ohka's luck changed. A sortie by eight Ohka/Isshiki combinations saw the picket destroyer USS *Mannert Abele* struck by an A6M5 Zero and then by an Ohka piloted by Lt Saburo Doi, which broke

The Ohka Model 22 was designed to be launched by the smaller but faster P1Y1 Ginga bomber, as shown in this illustration. (Author)

the ship in half, making the destroyer the first US ship sunk by an Ohka. The destroyer USS *Stanley* was hit and damaged during the same attack. The Ohka raids continued sporadically, with mixed results. Sorties by six bombers on April 16 were ineffective, but a transport and a destroyer were hit and damaged on May 4 and May 11. A final attack on June 22 by six bombers was wiped out by US fighters before reaching its target.

Japanese jet and rocket propulsion was heavily dependent on German technology. These are three of the engines intended for various kamikaze aircraft, starting with the Maru Ka-10 copy of the Argus As 0014 pulse-jet on the left (intended for the Baika), the Mitsubishi KR-10 rocket engine copied from the Walter HWK 109-509 (for the Shusui) fighter, and the NE-20 based on the BMW-003 (for the Kikka fighter and the Ohka Model 43). (NARA)

In total, 74 Ohka/Isshiki sorties were conducted during the Okinawa campaign, and 56 Ohka were either released or shot down while still attached to their parent bomber. These attacks sank the destroyer *Mannert Abele* and damaged at least two other destroyers. Aside from the vulnerability of the Ohka/Isshiki combination, the Ohka was very difficult to steer in its terminal dive, and there are numerous accounts of Ohka missing their targets. Following its combat use in the spring of 1945, there were about 230 Ohka Type 11 still in inventory in July, these being hoarded for the final defense of Japan.

Japan also acquired engineering information on the German Fieseler Fi-103 (V-1) "Buzz Bomb" cruise missile, and had begun to manufacture its Argus pulse-jet engine as the Maru Ka-10. Such pulse-jets were much easier to manufacture than axial-flow turbojets such as the Ne-20, and Japan attempted to acquire engineering drawings of the Fi-103 for production of a manned suicide version. Only a portion of the documentation arrived, so the IJN sponsored the development of the similar Baika (Plum Blossom), starting in the summer of 1945. Both the Yokosuka arsenal and Kawanishi offered designs, but neither had progressed beyond preliminary sketches before the war ended.

The Nakajima Kikka (Orange Blossom) was patterned after the German Me-262, but was somewhat smaller. There was controversy over its intended use, with some navy commanders urging its application as a fast bomber, even though it was nominally part of the Tokko aircraft program. It flew only once prior to war's end, due to delays with the associated Ne-20 turbojet engine effort. (NARA)

Planned Tokko Aircraft Production in 1945									
	May	Jun	Jul	Aug	Sep	Oct	Nov	Dec	Total
Ohka Type 22	6	49	30	50	60	60	60		315
Ohka Type 43			2	10	22	38	65	80	217
Ki-115/Toka	110	210	220	277	325	430*	500*	500*	2572
Total	116	259	252	337	407	528	625	580	3104

*Still under discussion

Special Attack Aircraft – The Ki-115 Tsuragi

The declining inventories of suitable suicide aircraft convinced the IJA to initiate its own program for a dedicated Tokko aircraft. In contrast to the navy's high-tech jet and rocket approach, the IJA favored low-tech solutions. In January 1945, the IJA started the Ki-115 Tsurugi (Sword) Experimental Army Special Attack Aircraft, which was a joint venture by the Mitaka Research Institute and the Nakajima plant at Ota. The aircraft was of very conventional design, and powered by a Nakajima Ha-115-II 1,130hp (843kW) radial engine. To simplify production, the aircraft used a basic, fixed landing gear and the tray for the bomb under the aircraft lacked any means to jettison the ordnance in the event that the mission had to be aborted.

The first prototype was completed on March 5, 1945, and began flight trials. The initial design proved to be too crude. The simple undercarriage made it difficult to handle the aircraft on the ground, visibility from the cockpit was poor, the wings were too small for adequate lift, and the lack of flaps aggravated its shortcomings during take-off. As a result, a re-design was ordered prior to series production. The first prototype of the revised Ki-115 Ko design was ready in June 1945, and it was rushed into production at Nakajima's plants at Iwate and Ota.

The IJA began a training program for Ki-115 pilots in late June 1945, but the program was abruptly cancelled after many pilots were killed flying the primitive aircraft. In spite of its shortcomings, the IJN saw the merits of the low-tech concept and approached Nakajima about building a similar

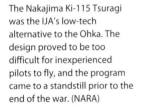

The Nakajima Ki-115 Tsuragi was the IJA's low-tech alternative to the Ohka. The design proved to be too difficult for inexperienced pilots to fly, and the program came to a standstill prior to the end of the war. (NARA)

aircraft designated as the Toka (Wisteria) for its own kamikaze units. The IJN expected to build thousands of Toka in 1945, more than the rest of its high-tech kamikaze aircraft combined. Its aircraft differed in the type of powerplant and the ability to drop the bomb in case of mission abort. In the event, no navy Ki-115s were ever built and none of the 104 Ki-115 Ko manufactured for the army were actually issued to combat units, due to the type's flying deficiencies. It is worth noting that a number of other cheap Tokko aircraft were under development at war's end, such as the elementary Ta Go (Bamboo Spear), which was of wooden construction and even simpler than the Tsuragi. However, most of these designs never left the drawing board or existed only in prototype form at the end of the war.

AERIAL KAMIKAZE

Japan lacked modern high-altitude interceptors, and when B-29 attacks against Japan began in the summer of 1944, there were suggestions of beginning aerial ramming attacks, sometimes called *Tai-atari* (Body Slamming). The first such aerial attack took place on August 7, 1944. The 10th Air Division in the Tokyo area set up a Tokko unit in October 1944 and their missions were successful enough that all units except for the 17th and 18th Air Regiments were ordered to assign three or four of their planes to a special *Shinten* (Heaven Quake) unit. A US assessment counted nine B-29s destroyed and 13 damaged by ramming at a cost of 21 Japanese fighters.

Another method to counter American air power was to attack the US aircraft bases. (Other Japanese paratrooper missions against US airfields are detailed in Osprey Elite 127, *Japanese Paratroop Forces of World War II.*) The IJA set up a number of special air raider units with plans to crash-land them at key American airbases, where the raiders would plant explosive charges to demolish aircraft and fuel dumps. During the 1945 missions, there were no plans for the commandos to escape.

The Giretsu (Gallantry) Airborne Unit was formed in the autumn of 1944 to attack B-29 bases in the Marianas. The planned January 1945 Marianas mission was cancelled when forward bases on Iwo Jima were damaged, but in May 1945 the target shifted to US bases recently established around Yontan on Okinawa. Operation *Gi* was launched on May 24, with Type 97 ("Sally") bombers as transports. Several aircraft returned to base with engine problems, and seven reached Okinawa, with 98 personnel. Some of these aircraft were shot down during the approaches to the runways, and the rest crash-landed before midnight. A handful of commando teams survived the

This Type 97 bomber was one of the aircraft converted into a transport for the Giretsu Airborne Unit that attacked US airbases near Yontan on Okinawa as part of Operation *Gi* on the night of May 24, 1945. The commandos emerging from this aircraft were relatively successful, causing considerable damage at the airbase before being killed. (NARA)

crash-landings and staged their attacks, destroying nine aircraft, damaging 29, and setting off a major blaze in the fuel dump. All of the 69 commandos and aircrew who disembarked were killed or committed suicide.

The IJN also planned Operation *Ken* against the Marianas bases using 300 troops of the Special Naval Landing Force carried by 30 Betty bombers. US forces, however, discovered the plan from radio intercepts and the transport force was destroyed at Misawa airbase by a US carrier air strike on July 14, 1945. At least two other large raids were ready in August 1945, including an IJA attack using gliders, but the war ended before they took place.

TOKKO NAVAL CRAFT: HUMAN TORPEDOES

The concept of a human-guided torpedo that could be launched underwater from a submarine was first proposed in Japan by junior officers of the midget submarine force at the Kure Navy Yard in 1942, but was rejected. One of these officers, Lt (jg) Hiroshi Kuroki, made a formal presentation to the Naval Technical Staff in Tokyo in February 1944, and under the worsening circumstances, the concept received more serious consideration.

Design work on a human torpedo began in March 1944 at Kure under the direction of Capt K. Mimizuka as the Kaiten Type 1. Kaiten was a contraction of the phrase "Kaiten igyo" or "Great Undertaking." The Kaiten was essentially a conversion of the Type 93 Model 3 "Long Lance" torpedo with an enlarged forward section to accommodate a single pilot and a massive 3,410lb (1,550kg) warhead. In contrast to some earlier manned torpedoes, such as the Italian Chariot, the pilot sat within the pressure hull, not as a frogman riding outside the torpedo. The first Kaiten Type 1 was completed at the Kure Naval Yard in June 1944 and began trials.

The intention was to develop a weapon that could be carried into the combat zone by a parent submarine, then launched from underwater. Later in the war, plans were also underway to deploy Kaiten from amphibious landing ships and also from shore installations. The main attraction of the Kaiten over a conventional torpedo was that the range was extended, the warhead was more powerful, and the guidance was expected to be more precise. Manufacture of the Kaiten Type 1 began in August 1944 at the Kure Navy Yard, and later at the Yokosuka and Hikari yards. Total production was about 330 Kaiten consisting of about 100 of the original Type 1 in 1944 and 230 of the improved Type 1 Mod 1 in 1945.

Various improvements were incorporated into the weapon during the course of production to remedy flaws discovered during training and operations. The most serious problem was the damage caused by leaks. Typically, the parent submarines traveled the first few days on the surface, but would then submerge when entering areas where US ships were active. It was during the submerged portion of the trip that the leakage issues became most serious. Although a number of changes were made in hopes of stopping

 KI-115 KO TSURAGI

The Nakajima Ki-115 Tsuragi was the army's low-cost, low-tech alternative to the navy's Ohka special attack aircraft. Unlike the Ohka, it used a simple aircraft configuration and so did not require a parent aircraft for launch. The prototype aircraft had a somewhat different undercarriage, and this illustration shows the production Ki-115 Ko configuration with the reinforced undercarriage. Due to lingering technical problems, no Tsuragi were issued to combat units, so no unit markings were carried.

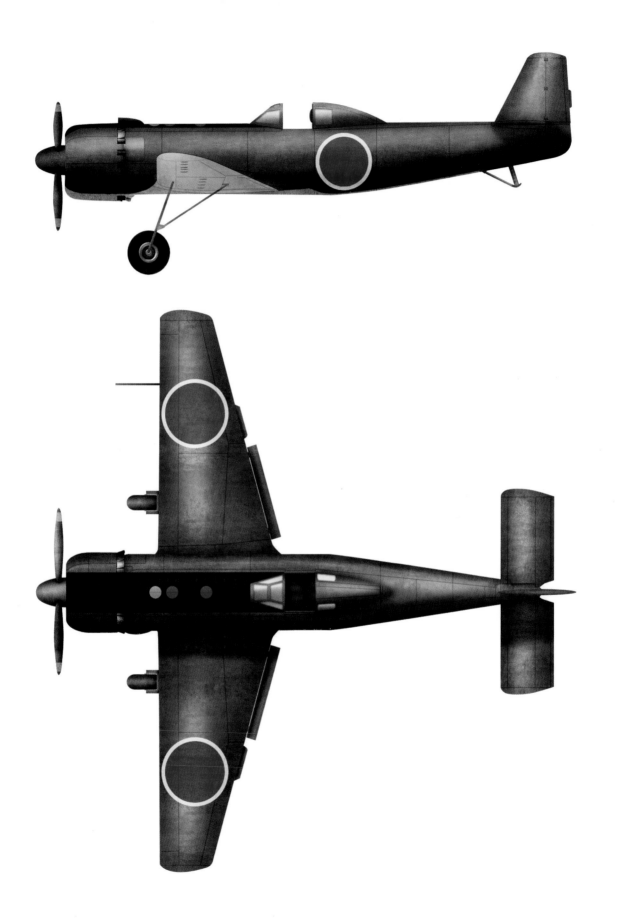

The Kaiten were manufactured at the Kure, Yokosuka, and Hikari navy yards; here is was one of the assembly areas at Yokosuka at the end of the war, with several camouflaged Kaiten Type 1 seen on rail-trolleys. (NARA)

this problem, leakage remained an issue through the war, often rendering the Kaiten inoperable.

The Kaiten were operated by 18–20-year-old volunteers, mainly reservists and petty officers from the navy aviation training groups. The 1st Special Submarine Training Base Group was established at Otsujima on Tokuyama Bay on July 10, 1944, under the command of Rear Adm Mitsuri Nagai. The initial training was conducted using modified Shinyo (Ocean Quake) crash boats configured so that the pilot had to use a periscope and magnetic compass for steering. After this training was complete, the trainees transitioned to modified Kaiten, which had an exercise warhead substituted for the real one.

The parent submarines were modified for the deployment role with a special watertight tunnel through the deck into the belly hatch on the Kaiten, so that the pilot could be transferred into the Kaiten during the underwater approach to the target. In practice, some of the initial conversions lacked this feature, so the submarine had to surface to transfer the pilot aboard. The Kaiten could operate to depths of about 200ft (60m), and during the terminal approach the pilot usually leveled off around 16ft (5m) in order to use the periscope. It had a maximum underwater speed of about 30 knots (34.5mph/55.5km/h).

The Kaiten Type 1 was not entirely satisfactory due to its elementary design, and the IJN decided to start design of a much more sophisticated version, the Type 2, through a collaborative effort between the IJN's Kure Torpedo Department and Mitsubishi's Nagasaki-Heiki facility. Its revolutionary Type 6 powerplant was influenced by German hydrogen-peroxide torpedo engines, and a variety of configurations were developed and tested. A pair of Type 2 were completed in December 1944, but the advanced propulsion system never proved practical and the project was abandoned. Instead, it was reconfigured as the Kaiten Type 4 in January–March 1945, but using a more conventional kerosene/oxygen torpedo engine. Although the expected top speed of the Kaiten 4 was 40 knots (46mph/74km/h), trials indicated it could barely make 20 knots (23mph/37km/h), even though it was lighter than the Kaiten Type 2. A total of five Kaiten Type 4 were built before the program was abandoned. The Kaiten Type 10 was a reversion to the original Kaiten Type 1 idea, but based on the smaller Type 92 electric torpedo. It was a far simpler conversion than the Type 1, but also considerably more limited in performance, with only a 660lb (300kg) warhead. It had not entered production before the end of the war and only about six were completed.

Kaiten Operations

The Kaiten operations were codenamed *Gen* and were scheduled to begin in September 1944 against US Navy anchorages because these contained a large volume of relatively static targets. Due to delays in manufacturing and training, the first *Gen* operation did not leave Otsujima until November 8, 1944, consisting of three submarines each with four Kaiten. Submarine I-37 was sunk by US warships on November 19, 1944, before launching its Kaiten, but I-36 and I-47 managed to release all eight of their Kaiten on November 20, 1944, outside Ulithi Atoll. Many of the Kaiten were spotted and sunk, but one struck the fleet oiler *Mississinewa*, which led to a massive fire due to its cargo of aviation fuel. The parent submarines spotted the enormous column of smoke over the harbor and assumed that several ships had been sunk.

The exaggerated assessment of the first raid encouraged the dispatch of a second Kaiten operation, which departed the Inland Sea on New Year's Day and included I-36 and I-48 heading to Ulithi, I-47 to Hollandia, I-53 to Palau,

An enormous plume of smoke marks the sinking of the oiler USS *Mississinewa* by a Kaiten on November 20, 1944, at Ulithi Atoll, as seen from the bridge of battleship USS *North Carolina*. The apparent success of this attack encouraged a costly but largely futile Kaiten campaign over the next few months. (NARA)

The crew wave from on top of their Kaiten submarines as they depart on the *Kikusui* 3 mission on February 21, 1945 from Hikari harbor. The I-370 was a Type D-1 Tei-Gata class transport submarine converted to the Kaiten role in January 1945. It was lost on this mission when depth-charged by the destroyer USS *Finnegan* near Iwo Jima on February 26, 1945. As is typical of a submarine on a Kaiten mission, it has the *Kikusui* marking painted on the conning tower.

I-56 to the Admiralties, and I-58 to Guam, with all attacks scheduled for "X Day" – January 12, 1945. I-48 was sunk before it reached its destination, but the other submarines launched their attacks and reported large numbers of explosions and smoke columns. In fact, no Kaiten had succeeded, but Tokyo assessed the results as 18 ships destroyed, including carriers, battleships, and transports. The exaggerated assessments of these two missions led to plans to shift most of IJN submarine operations to Kaiten missions over the next few months.

The next *Gen* operation – off Iwo Jima in February 1945 – was hastily improvised and led to the loss of several of the participating submarines and a cancellation of the operation on March 6. Another *Gen* mission was dispatched in March during the Okinawa campaign using four submarines, but once again it was ineffective due to vigorous US Navy anti-submarine tactics. This failure led to a strenuous debate within the IJN over whether the primary targets of the Kaiten should be ships at anchorage or ships on the open sea; subsequent missions began to shift towards the latter. An operation into the Philippine Sea in July 1945 scored the last Kaiten victory, when the destroyer escort USS *Underhill* was blown in half by a Kaiten launched by I-53. In total, the IJN's 6th Fleet conducted eight major and two minor Kaiten

 KAITEN TYPE 1 SUBMARINE

The Kaiten shown here is in training markings with the upper portion of the hull painted in white. It also carries the *Kikusui* marking insignia adopted by the Kaiten Corps. The combat Kaiten seldom carried markings and were painted in black for camouflage. The training Kaiten had an exercise warhead, fitted in place of the normal warhead and of the same shape and weight.

Key

1. Inertial pistol for warhead detonation
2. Main warhead
3. Electric detonator
4. Air chamber tanks for steering
5. Type 93 torpedo oxygen vessel
6. Forward trim tank
7. Lower hatch for connection to parent submarine

8. Electric gyroscope for steering
9. Rear trim tank
10. Type 93 Model 1 torpedo propulsion system
11. Periscope
12. Upper hatch
13. Pilot
14. Steering rudder

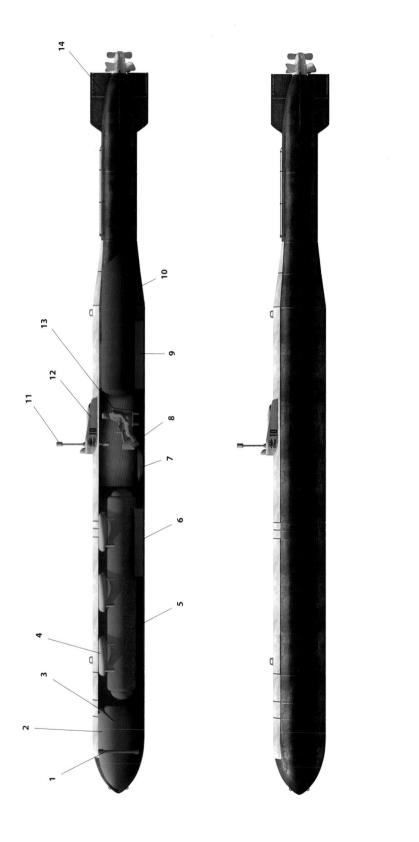

One of the last submarine Tokko attacks underway in the final days of the war was Operation *Arashi* (Storm), an attempt to launch suicide aircraft against the US fleet anchorage at Ulithi Atoll in August 1945. The large submarines I-400 and I-401 were originally intended for attacks on the Panama Canal using their Seiran aircraft, but the assignment was changed on June 25, 1945. The war ended before the operation was carried out, and here the submarines are seen tied up alongside the USS *Proteus* in Yokosuka harbor on September 7, 1945, with their capacious aircraft hanger doors open in front of the conning tower. I-14, in the foreground, was supposed to deliver scout planes to Truk in advance of the main attack. (NARA)

operations, losing four fleet submarines and four transport submarines. A total of 147 Kaiten were dispatched on these missions, of which 79 were launched in combat. They sank two US ships and possibly hit or damaged five or six more.

Kaiten Missions, 1944–45					
Mission	**Date**	**Submarines**	**Kaiten group**	**Kaiten embarked**	**Kaiten launched**
Gen 1	Nov 11, 1944	I-36, I-37, I-47	Kikusui	12	8
Gen 2	Dec 19, 1944	I-36, I-47, I-48, I-53, I-57, I-58	Kongo	24	19
Gen 3	Feb 20, 1945	I-44, I-368, I-370	Chihaya	14	10
Gen 4	Mar 1–2, 1945	I-36, I-58	Kamitake	8	0
Gen 5	Mar 29–31, 1945	I-44, I-47, I-56, I-58	Tatara	20	10
Gen 6	Apr 20, 1945	I-36, I-47	Amatake/Tembu	12	8
	May 5, 1945	I-367		5	2
Gen 7	May 24–Jun 15, 1945	I-36, I-165, I-361, I-363	Todoroki	18	10
Gen 8	Jul 14–Aug 8, 1945	I-47, I-53, I-58, I-363, I-366, I-367	Tamon	32	12
	Aug 16, 1945	I-159		2	0

Midget Submarines

The IJN had used midget submarines since the beginning of the war, for example in the Pearly Harbor attack. Two types of midget coastal defense submarines were allotted to the Tokko mission in 1944. The Koryu and Kairyu were both designed to carry two torpedoes: the Koryu carried them stacked one above the other in bow launch tubes, while the Kairyu had the torpedoes externally mounted on the lower hull casing. Although they could fire their torpedoes and escape, they were expected to use ramming tactics to ensure the destruction of the target ship. The Koryu was considered the most

One of the more common Tokko submarines was the Koryu Type D; there were plans to complete 570 by the end of September 1945 at the Yokosuka navy yard. It had a crew of five and was armed with two 45cm torpedoes stacked one atop each other in the bow. (NARA)

effective Tokko submarine, with an anticipated exchange ratio of two ships sunk for every three Koryus, compared to only 1:3 for Kaitens and Kairyus. A total of about 110 Kairyus and 250 Koryus were built by the end of the war, but they were reserved for the final Operation *Ketsu-Go* and so did not see combat use.

IJN Tokko Naval Weapon Production in 1945							
	April	May	June	April–June (sub-total)	April–June (planned)	July–September 1945 (planned)	October 1945–March 1946 (planned)
Small submarines	0	2	2	4	6	14	20
Koryu	12	12	20	44	110	430	1,000
Kairyu	9	42	74	125	300	550	1,000
Kaiten	66	42	51	159	250		
Shinyo Type 1	68	316	284	668	1,200	1,350	1,000
Shinyo Type 5	181	167	111	459	450	900	200

Crash Boats

As in the case of the human torpedoes, the development of crash boats began in the spring of 1944 with separate army and navy programs. The IJN program was overseen by the 4th Section (Ship Construction) of the Navy Technical Department in Tokyo, which assigned it to Capt S. Makino at the Yokosuka navy yard. The design was a scaled-down version of existing 59ft (18m) motor torpedo boats. The intention was to develop a very simple design that could be produced in large numbers using automobile engines. Two configurations were built in prototype form, six steel prototypes at Yokosuka, and two wooden prototypes at the nearby Tsurumi yard. The first Shinyo boats were completed on May 27, 1944, and put through trials. The steel hull had strength issues and, furthermore, the wooden type was far easier to manufacture so it was selected for production. The original Shinyo Type 1 used a transmission between the engine and the propeller that was costly and in short supply. This led to its redesign as the Shinyo Type 1 Mod 1, which dropped the transmission and reoriented the engine to drive the propeller shaft directly. The Mod 1 boat was smaller than the original 19ft 8in (6m) design – only 16ft 9in (5.1m) – and it became the predominant production type in 1944.

The Shinyo Type 1 Mod 1 was powered by a Toyota KC 6 cylinder automobile engine and had a speed of 23 knots (26.5mph/42.6km/h). Its principal weapon was a 595lb (270kg) charge of Type 98 high explosive in the bow, which could be detonated by an impact fuze or a manual switch. Production of these boats was undertaken at several navy shipyards, private yards, and also at a number of automobile plants. As a result, there were many small design differences between the boats built at different factories. Initial combat deployments led to a number of suggestions for improvements. One of the first changes was to incorporate a simple rocket launcher on the stern, one that could fire the standard naval 12cm shrapnel-incendiary rocket. The launcher had several roles: partly to distract US Navy gunners, partly to give the Shinyo pilot a bit of courage during the approach when under fire, and finally to cause some harm to the target ship before impact. The

F **KAITEN PATROL OFF IWO JIMA, JULY 1945**

I-58 was a B-3 class submarine launched in June 1943 and attached to the Kure Naval District. In September 1944, it was modified to carry four Kaiten. Commanded by LtCdr Matsushiro Hashimoto, it first saw combat as part of the Kongo (Diamond) Group against Apra harbor on Guam. All four Kaiten were launched on January 12, 1945, but one exploded prematurely; two pillars of smoke were spotted and I-58 was erroneously credited with an escort carrier and an oiler, though no US ships were in fact sunk by Kaiten. In March 1945, I-58 was committed to the Iwo Jima campaign, but diverted to take part in Operation *Tan No. 2*, the air attack on the Ulithi Atoll, with the submarine serving as a radio beacon. After returning to Japan for more Kaiten training, I-58 departed Kure in late March on Operation *Gen 5* as part of the Tatara Group to attack US shipping off Okinawa. I-58 was unsuccessful in its missions there, as it was repeatedly forced to submerge due to the presence of US aircraft. After returning to Kure, the submarine was heavily reconfigured by removing its aircraft hanger to permit it to carry six Kaiten as well as fitting a snorkel to permit undersea cruising to avoid US aircraft; the illustration here shows this final configuration.

I-58 set out on its most eventful Kaiten mission on July 16, 1945, as part of the Tamon Group with five other submarines, with plans to attack US shipping off the Philippines. On July 28, two Kaiten were launched, one against the armed merchantman SS *Wild Hunter* and the other against its escort, the USS *Lowry*. The *Lowry* engaged one Kaiten with its deck gun and rammed the other. On July 29, 1945, while north of Palau, I-58 picked up a large warship that it misidentified as a battleship. It was in fact the cruiser USS *Indianapolis* on its way back from the Marianas after delivering the nuclear materiel for the Hiroshima and Nagasaki atomic bombs. Hashimoto decided that the Kaitens would not be able to acquire the ship in the dark and so attacked it with conventional torpedoes. The *Indianapolis* was struck and sank shortly after midnight. Due to the secrecy of its mission, the loss of the *Indianapolis* was not realized for days and many of its surviving crewman died in the water from shark attack. Hashimoto continued his mission and on August 9, 1945, attacked a hunter-killer team of Task Group 75.19 led by CVE-96 USS *Salamaua*. The submarine attempted to launch three Kaiten, but two proved faulty and only two were dispatched. US sailors initially mistook the Kaiten for whales, but when identified one was sunk by gunfire and the other by depth charges. On August 12, one Kaiten was launched from a range of about 9,850yds (9,000m) against USS *Oak Hill* (LSD-7), but the Kaiten was spotted by the dock landing ship's escort, the USS *T.F. Nickels* (DE-587), which rammed it. The Kaiten escaped, but surfaced shortly afterwards and the pilot, Hayashi Toshiaki, set off the warhead. I-58 returned to Kure and was surrendered at the end of the war.

The precise markings and color of I-58 on its July mission remain obscure. Many Kaiten submarines carried the *Kikusui* emblem on their conning towers. Other markings also included a Japanese flag and the ship number, but these were often painted on canvas banners that could be attached in home waters and then removed during the patrol. Japanese submarines were initially finished in the usual IJN dark gray, but by the later stage of the war, were usually painted overall black with red-lead antifouling paint on the lower hull. A band of black anti-sonar paint was painted 3–5ft (0.9–1.5m) wide near the waterline.

The Kairyu was a small, two-man Tokko submarine that could carry either two torpedoes externally or be fitted with an explosive contact charge in the bow. It was inexpensively made, being powered by an Isuzu automobile engine. These examples are seen in Yokosuka harbor, where 207 were built. (NARA)

boats were fitted with either one or two launchers. After initial combat employment in the Philippines in the autumn of 1944, recommendations were made to include a net cutter on the front of the boat to handle protective booms. This system usually included a cable cutter on the bow, another cutter in front of the cockpit, and a deflector in front of the propeller to prevent the blade from becoming entangled in lines. These cutters varied in design from yard to yard and were added from the spring of 1945. The IJN planned to build about 7,000 Shinyo boats by September 1945, and some 6,200 were completed before the end of the war, not only in Japan, but in Singapore, China, and the Dutch East Indies.

A number of more elaborate Shinyo boat designs were undertaken in Yokosuka, the focus being on developing faster and more survivable boats. These included hydrofoil designs and even rocket-powered boats. None of these designs proved practical, however. The only other major type built during the war was the Shinyo Type 5, which was intended to serve as a detachment leader's boat and so it was fitted with two engines and carried a 13mm heavy machine gun. The idea was that this boat would lead the attack, and provide covering fire for the rest of the detachment. The first of these was completed in August 1944 and went into production in the autumn.

This Shinyo Type 1 Mod 4 was part of the Kawatana Assault Group in Ogushi harbor near Sasebo on Kyushu. It is fitted with a single 12cm rocket launcher on the starboard stern and has a cable cutter on the bow. (NARA)

The Type 5 was a detachment leader boat and was larger than the Type 1. It could be fitted with a 13mm machine gun in front of the cabin, but that is absent on this boat, which had been disarmed prior to the US occupation. This boat was part of the Kawatana Assault Group in Ogushi harbor. (NARA)

The Army Renraku-tei Boats

The IJA had a parallel boat program that was a local initiative by LtGen Yoshiaburo Suzuki from the Shipping Engineers at Ujina, a branch that was responsible for army logistics in the Pacific. In March 1944, he proposed arming small boats with explosives and other weapons to conduct fast raids against invading American amphibious forces. There was still some ambivalence about suicide tactics when the proposal was first made, so the initial idea was to build a boat that could carry a pair of 264lb (120kg) Model 98 depth charges on the stern, which could be rolled off near American landing craft. They would also have an explosive charge that could be detonated on impact or with a time fuze so that the pilot could escape. The boat was designed by the army's research institute at Himeji near Kobe and tested in Tokyo harbor in June 1944. The crash boats were given the cover name of Renraku-tei (Liaison Boats) or Maru-ni (Large Boats), while the associated sea raiding regiments used the cover name of Akatsuki (Dawn) Regiments. The Renraku-tei boats were similar in overall design to the IJN Shinyo boats and were powered by 85hp (63kW) automobile engines. Boat construction, along with the formation of the first sea-raiding regiments, began in September 1944. The crews were recruited from young

This comparison photo from the stern shows the difference between the Type 1 (left) and Type 5 (right) Shinyo boats. The Type 1 had a single pilot while the Type 5 had a crew of two with a second sailor manning the 13mm machine gun. (NARA)

16–17-year-old officer cadets who were posthumously advanced to the rank of lieutenant after their mission. Each regiment included three boats companies and a total of 100 boats, including the reserve. By the time these boats were deployed in early 1945, the inhibitions over suicide tactics had evaporated and usually they were used as crash boats like the navy Shinyo vessels.

The army Renraku-tei boats can be distinguished from the navy Shinyo by the claw-shaped rack on the stern on either corner, which carried the boat's depth charge. This particular boat was captured on Aka Shima during the Okinawa campaign. (NARA)

Initial Boat Combat

The first IJN Shinyo units were raised at Sasebo in the summer of 1944 in squadron strength, with each unit consisting of about 200 men and 48 boats. Shinyo Squadrons 1 through 5 were sent to Chichijima and Hahajima in the Bonin Islands, while Shinyo Squadrons 6 to 13 were sent to the Philippines and headquartered at Corregidor. The navy units in the Philippines were reinforced by army Akatsuki regiments with 800 Renraku-tei boats deployed around the Lingayen Gulf, Manila Bay, Batangas, and Lamon Bay on Luzon. Numerous boats were lost during the transfers from Japan and through initial US naval bombardments of key ports and bases. The first attempted attack by Shinyo Squadron 9 ended in disaster when a fire on one of the boats spread among the craft while still in harbor, leading to the detonation of a few warheads, which wiped out the unit. The army was the next to try, with an attack by Akatsuki Regiments 11 and 12 in the Lingayen Gulf in the pre-dawn hours of January 10, 1945. One or more of the army boats executed a depth charge attack on the Landing Ship, Tank LST-925, severely damaging one engine. Four LST and eight transport ships were rammed and damaged by crash boats, but the only vessels sunk were two Landing Craft, Infantry (LCI) vessels modified as gunboats. The Akatsuki units expended 45 boats in the attack, and believed that they had sunk or seriously damaged 20–30 US ships.

The US Navy responded by deploying the "Cactus Navy," a flotilla of gun-armed PT boats that conducted raids against known Japanese bases, as well as the nightly "Flycatcher" patrol tasked with intercepting the crash boats. The crash boat bases were also struck by aircraft, destroying or damaging many of the craft. US Navy tactics indeed prevented any mass attacks, but sporadic operations continued. Sub-chaser PC-1129 tried attacking a crash boat flotilla around midnight on January 31, 1945, but was rammed and sunk. By mid February 1945, only about 60 of the original

G **SHINYO TYPE 1 MOD 4 CRASH BOAT**
This version of the Shinyo crash boat, the Type 1 Mod 4, entered widespread production in the spring of 1945. By this stage, it has the full complement of improvements, such as the 12cm rocket launchers and the cable cutters. These crash boats received various paint schemes, a dark green with red-lead anti-fouling paint underneath being one of the more common schemes.

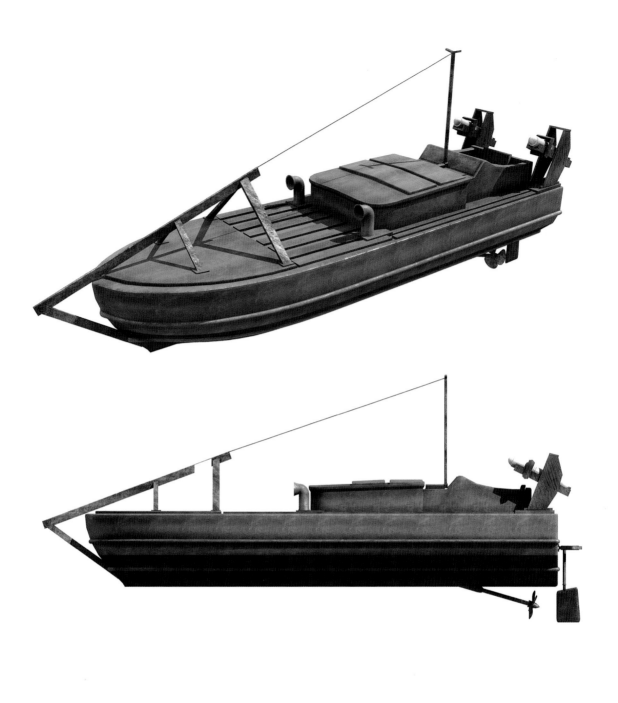
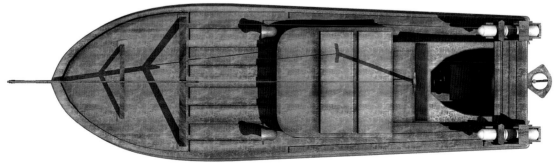

A US infantryman inspects one of the Renraku-tei crash boats discovered near the shore on Okinawa during the fighting there in the spring of 1945. (NARA)

1,200 crash boats were still operational, and on the night of February 15, the surviving IJN units on Corregidor staged a final attack after dark against a barrier of gun-armed Landing Craft, Support (LCS) vessels at the mouth of the Mariveles anchorage, sinking three craft and damaging another.

Two of the IJN Shinyo squadrons in the Bonin Islands were moved to Iwo Jima prior to the US attack on the island, but were overwhelmed by preparatory naval gunfire. Seven IJA Akatsuki regiments and more than 700 boats were also deployed to the Okinawa area in early 1945 on Kerama Retto and the neighboring islands under the command of the 5th Sea Raiding Base Headquarters. The 1st, 2nd, and 3rd Sea Raiding Regiments on the islands were mostly overrun by US forces, which took the Kerama chain in late March 1945 as a preliminary step to the main assault on Okinawa. A few boats were launched with no effect, and most of the 250 vessels there were scuttled or burned by their units.

On Okinawa itself, the IJN deployed the 22nd and 42nd Shinyo Squadrons in addition to the four IJA Akatsuki regiments. The IJN boats attempted a sortie on the evening of March 29, 1945, with no effect, but a March 31 attack by about 50 Renraku-tei boats sank the LSM-12 landing ship. An attack by four surviving IJN boats of Shinyo Squadron 22 on the night of April 3 also sank the gunboat LCI(G)-82.

During the first week of fighting around Okinawa, LCI gunboats claimed to have sunk 71 Japanese explosive motor boats (EMBs). Actions around the port of Naha were so frequent that the US Navy kept the harbor illuminated at night with star shells for most of the month to deter EMB attacks. There were sporadic assaults by the army's 27th, 28th, and 29th Akatsuki Regiments in April, seriously damaging the destroyer USS *Hutchins* and an LCI gunboat on April 27, and damaging several other ships and craft on other occasions. By early May, the attrition of the boats had been so severe that there were only infrequent scattered attacks, and attempts to reinforce the Okinawa garrison with boat detachments from Taiwan were frustrated when their transport ships were bombed.

Tokko Craft in the Final Defense of Japan

In the wake of the Philippines and Okinawa campaigns, control of both the army Renraku-tei and Shinyo crash boats came under IJN control. The IJN decided to unify the coastal defense Tokko units into assault groups that contained a mixed assortment of midget submarines, manned torpedoes, and crash boats. These were concentrated in the Kyushu and Tokyo areas, where the main US amphibious landings were expected.

IJN Tokkotai Assault Groups in Western Japan, July 1945					
Assault Groups	Location	Shinyo	Renraku-tei	Kaiten	Koryu/Kairyu
	Kyushu				
32 AG	Kagoshima Bay	500	200		12
Kawatana AG	Nagasaki	200	100		
31 AG	Goto Archipelago	50		4	
34 AG	Fukuoka	25	100		
24 AG	Saiki				12
35 AG	Hyuga Sea	125	100	2	
33 AG	Shibushi Bay	100	200	34	12
101/102 AG	Bungo Strait				18
	Shikoku				
21 AG	Sukumo Bay	50		8	12
23 AG	Tosa Bay	175		24	
	Honshu				
36 AG	Tsushima Strait				2
22 AG	Kii Strait	24		4	50
Sub-total (deployed)		1,249	700	76	118
Total (inc. reserve)		2,150	700	119	125

During the *Ketsu-Go* operation, the IJN Tokko weapons were intended to provide layered defense. The Koryu submarines were expected to carry out the attacks furthest from shore during the initial approach of the US fleet, and these would be followed by actions of the shorter-ranged Kairyu submarines. By this stage in the war, there was little confidence in the Kaiten submarines, based on past performance, and they were intended for use primarily from shore bases against US ships engaging in shore bombardment or against US transports. The Shinyo crash boats were to be committed against transport ships anchored off shore and, again in view of recent experience, they were supposed to be reserved for operations at night or in obscured weather conditions, due to their vulnerability. An IJN report indicated that "The principal operational mission of these forces will be to shatter the enemy invaders at sea prior to landing." Navy officers expected an attack by about 2,000 transport ships and anticipated an attrition of about a quarter of this force, 470 ships, by the Tokko units, a tally consisting of about 210 transports likely to be sunk by kamikaze aircraft, and 260 by submarines and crash boats. The effectiveness of the Tokko vessels was expected to be about 2:3 for the Koryu, 1:3 for the Kaiten and Kairyu, and 1:10 for the Shinyo.

OTHER KAMIKAZE WEAPONS

Kamikaze Frogmen

In expectation of American landings in the Home Islands, the Yokosuka naval district began preparing close-combat Tokko frogmen units for destroying American landing craft on their approach to the beach. The Fukuryu (Crouching Dragon) were equipped with a special diving suit and breathing apparatus, of which about 1,000 were manufactured by August 1945, with a total of 8,000 planned by September 1945. The Coast Surprise Attack Force was intended to total 6,000 frogmen and to be ready for combat by October 1945.

The primary Fukuryu weapon was the Type 5 Attack Mine, which was a 22lb (10kg) explosive charge on the end of a long pole and fitted with a contact fuze. A Fukuryu defense position would start with a row of contact mines, tethered to the sea floor at a depth of 32–49ft (10–15m), which would be released by the Fukuryu frogmen to bob to the surface at the appropriate moment. Closer to shore were three rows of Fukuryu frogmen, with the rows 66yds (60m) apart and the frogmen in a line 55yds (50m) from each other. By staggering the rows, there would only be a maximum gap of 22yds (20m) for the approaching landing craft.

The intention was to deploy these forces in water about 13–20ft (4–6m) deep. The swimmers would thrust their Type 5 mines against the bottoms of landing craft as they approached overhead, hopefully sinking them. A variety of experiments were conducted to create "underwater foxholes" using concrete pipes or pre-fabricated concrete shelters to help shelter the Fukuryu frogmen from any American countermeasures, as well as to protect them from the blasts when nearby frogmen set off their lunge mines. The organization of the Fukuryu was based on a section of six frogmen, with five sections per platoon, five platoons per company, and three companies per battalion. The first Fukuryu unit was the 71st Totsugekitai Arashi (Special Attack Unit), raised in Yokosuka in the summer of 1945 with two battalions and a further four in training. Eventually, this formation was expected to deploy about 4,000 frogmen in the defense of Tokyo harbor and the invasion of the nearby Honshu beaches. The 81st Arashi at Kure and the Kawatana Arashi at Sasebo were intended to deploy 1,000 divers each. The IJN staff was very keen on the idea and wanted to deploy 40,000 frogmen for the final defense of Japan, but the plan was constrained by the lack of underwater equipment.

Army Kamikaze Weapons

One of the most challenging threats facing Japanese infantry in the Pacific fighting was the widespread use of M4 medium tanks by the US Army and the US Marine Corps. The Japanese infantry lacked an effective antitank weapon comparable to the German Panzerfaust or American bazooka. A variety of weapons were hastily deployed to deal with the tank threat, including the Type 99 magnetic demolition charge, and various satchel charges that could be thrown under tanks or onto their engine decks.

US Navy personnel inspect a group of Shinyo Type 1 boats near Nagasaki in September 1945, some of the 200 assigned to the Kawatana Assault Group. (NARA)

During the Philippines campaign in the autumn of 1944, the IJA 14th Army introduced the lunge mine. This was a shaped-charge warhead placed on the end of a long pole. The Japanese infantryman hid until a tank passed, then rushed out and pushed the mine against the tank. The impact detonated the charge, but the soldier was likely to be killed in the process. Another kamikaze tactic used in the Philippines as well as on Iwo Jima and Okinawa was the use of Nikaku "human mine" tactics, where a Japanese infantryman would carry a special back-pack mine on straps over his shoulders. He would approach the enemy tank, then throw himself between the tracks and pull a detonating cord, setting off the charge under the tank's hull.

Although Japanese close-range antitank efforts were quite effective in the 1945 fighting, most of the American tank casualties came from more conventional tactics including the co-ordinated use of mines, antitank guns, and other types of antitank weapons. There was at least one instance of the use of kamikaze tanks. In April 1945, when US forces were approaching the IJA headquarters in Baguio on Luzon, Gen Tomoyuki Yamashita ordered a kamikaze attack by fitting large explosive charges to the front of a Type 97 medium tank and Type 95 light tank, which were then camouflaged with brush while hidden along the road. When US M4 medium tanks appeared around a bend on Route 9 on the morning of April 17, the two Japanese tanks raced forward and rammed the enemy vehicles, but the charges failed to detonate.

3.34m

This wartime US Navy intelligence drawing shows the configuration of the Fukuryu frogman and his underwater breathing apparatus. The inset drawing to the right shows a cross-section of the Type 5 attack mine; the upper half contains the 22lb (10kg) explosive charge, while the lower part is a hollow float chamber. Below is a silhouette drawing showing the relative size of the Fukuryu frogman with his anti-craft lunge mine. (NARA)

FURTHER READING

The kamikaze have been a source of unending fascination and there are numerous accounts in Japanese, English, and other languages. The bibliography here covers mainly English-language accounts, but a few of the better-illustrated Japanese accounts such as the Model Art series are mentioned here for modelers. This book focuses mainly on the weapons used in the kamikaze missions, but there is an extensive literature both on the personal experiences of the Japanese caught up in the kamikaze movement, as well as numerous American accounts of the ships that were on the receiving end of the kamikaze attacks; some of these are listed here. Some lesser-known English sources on kamikaze operations are the numerous monographs that were prepared by Japanese officers under the direction of US occupation forces in Japan in the years after the war. These were produced with the aim of recreating an account of the Pacific War, in spite of the large-scale destruction of Japanese documents between the surrender and the start of US occupation; the MacArthur report is a related effort. The United States Strategic Bombing

Survey (USSBS) and Naval Technical Mission studies are more narrowly focused accounts, concentrating on industrial and technical issues relating to the kamikazes. The USSBS files at the National Archives and Records Administration (NARA) at College Park, Maryland, also contain extensive background material, such as a set of interrogations of senior IJA and IJN officers about the kamikaze operations. I also examined a variety of files at the National Air and Space Museum (NASM), especially those dealing with the restoration of the Ohka and the associated reports by Robert Mikesh. A particularly informative website on the subject is Bill Gordon's "Kamikaze Images" (wgordon.web.wesleyan.edu/kamikaze/index.htm).

Japanese Monographs
Philippines Air Operations Record – Phase III August 1944–February 1945 (No. 12)
Homeland Operations Record (No. 17)
Homeland Operations Record, Volume IV, Fifth Area Army, Late 1943–1945 (No. 21)
Air Defense of the Homeland, 1944–1945 (No. 23)
Okinawa Area Naval Operations January–June 1945 (No. 83)
Philippines Area Naval Operations Part II – October–December 1944 (No. 84)
Preparations for Operations in Navy Defense of the Homeland, Plans and Preparations, July 1944–July 1945 (No. 85)
5th Air Fleet Operations, February–August 1945 (No. 86)
Outline of Third Phase Operations, February 1943–August 1945 (No. 117)
Homeland Defense Naval Operations, Part II, March 1943–August 1945 (No. 123)
Homeland Defense Naval Operations, Part III, June 1944–August 1945 (No. 124)
Submarine Operations in Third Phase Operations, Parts III, IV, and V Defense Operations, March 1944–August 1945 (No. 184)

US Naval Technical Mission to Japan Reports
Japanese Torpedoes and Tubes: Article 1 – Ship and Kaiten Torpedoes (O-01-1, 1946)
Characteristics of Japanese Naval Vessels: Submarines (Supplement II, S-01-7, 1946)
Ship and Related Targets: Japanese Suicide Craft (S-02, 1946)
The Fukuryu Special Harbor Defense and Underwater Attack Unit – Tokyo Bay (S-91, 1946)

USSBS Reports
The Japanese Aircraft Industry (No. 15, 1947)
Japanese Air Power (No. 62, 1947)
Japanese Air Weapons and Tactics (No. 63, 1947)

Other US Government Reports
Defense against Kamikaze Attacks in World War II and its Relevance to Anti-ship Missile Defense (Center for Naval Analyses: November 1970)
German Technical Aid to Japan (Military Intelligence Division: August 1945)
Handbook on Guided Missiles: Germany and Japan, (Military Intelligence Division: February 1946)
Reports of General MacArthur: Japanese Operations in the Southwest Pacific Area Vol. II–Part II (Demobilization Bureau: 1966)

Books
n/a, *Ningen gyorai kaiten (Kaiten Human Torpedo)* (Mediason: 2006)
Adams, Andrew (ed.), *Born to Die: The Cherry Blossom Squadrons* (Ohara: 1973)

This illustration from a US Army technical intelligence bulletin during the Okinawa campaign shows the employment of a lunge mine. Japanese infantry was taught to push it against the thinner side armor of American tanks. The prongs at the front are intended to keep the warhead at the optimum distance for the detonation of its shaped-charge warhead. (MHI)

Grunden, Walter, *Secret Weapons & World War II: Japan in the Shadow of Big Science* (University Press of Kansas: 2005)

Inoguchi, Rikihei et al., *The Divine Wind* (US Naval Institute: 1958)

Ishiguro, Ryusuke and Tadeusz Januszewski, *Japanese Special Attack Aircraft & Flying Bombs* (Mushroom Press: 2009)

Lamont-Brown, Raymond, *Kamikaze: Japan's Suicide Samurai* (Arms & Armour: 1997)

Millot, Bernard, *Divine Thunder: The Life & Death of the Kamikazes* (McCall: 1970)

Nagatsuka, Ryugi, *I Was a Kamikaze* (Macmillan: 1972)

Naito, Hatsuho, *Thunder Gods: The Kamikaze Pilots Tell Their Story* (Kodansha: 1982)

O'Neill, Richard, *Suicide Squads*, (Salamander: 1981)

Rielly, Robin, *Kamikaze Attacks of World War II: A Complete History of Japanese Suicide Strikes on American Ships, by Aircraft and Other Means* (McFarland: 2010)

Sakaida, Henry et al., *I-400: Japan's Secret Aircraft-Carrying Strike Submarine* (Hikoki: 2006)

Sheftall, M.G., *Blossoms in the Wind: Human Legacies of the Kamikaze* (Penguin: 2005)

Stern, Robert, *Fire from the Sky: Surviving the Kamikaze Threat* (US Naval Institute: 2010)

Warner, Denis & Peggy, and Sadao Seno, *The Sacred Warriors* (Van Nostrand: 1982)

Yokota, Yutaka, *Suicide Submarine: The Story of Japan's Submarine Kamikaze of Manned Torpedoes* (Ballantine: 1962)

Magazine Special Issues

"Kamikaze," *Batailles Aeriennes Hors Serie*, No. 19 (2002)

"Okinawa: La Bataille des Kamikaze," *Airmag Hors Serie*, No. 2 (2005)

"Imperial Japanese Army Air Force Suicide Attack Unit," *Model Art Special*, No. 451 (1995)

"Imperial Japanese Navy Air Force Suicide Attack Unit 'Kamikaze,'" *Model Art Special*, No. 458 (1995)

INDEX

Note: numbers in **bold** refer to illustrations